solar system

MERCURY
AND
VENUS

Rosalind Mist

QEB Publishing

Words in **bold** can be found in the glossary on page 22.

Library of Congress Control Number: 2008012588

ISBN 978 1 59566 579 9

Printed and bound in the United States

Author Rosalind Mist
Consultant Terry Jennings
Editor Amanda Askew
Designer Melissa Alaverdy
Picture Researcher Maria Joannou
Illustrator Richard Burgess

Publisher Steve Evans
Creative Director Zeta Davies

Contents

The Solar System

The Solar System is made up of the Sun, and everything that orbits, **or circles, it.** This includes the planets and their moons, as well as **meteors, asteroids,** and **comets**.

Jupiter

Uranus

Neptune

Saturn

The Solar System is held together by an invisible force called **gravity**. On Earth, gravity stops people from floating into space!

When an **astronaut** is in orbit, they are freely falling around the Earth and feel weightless.

4

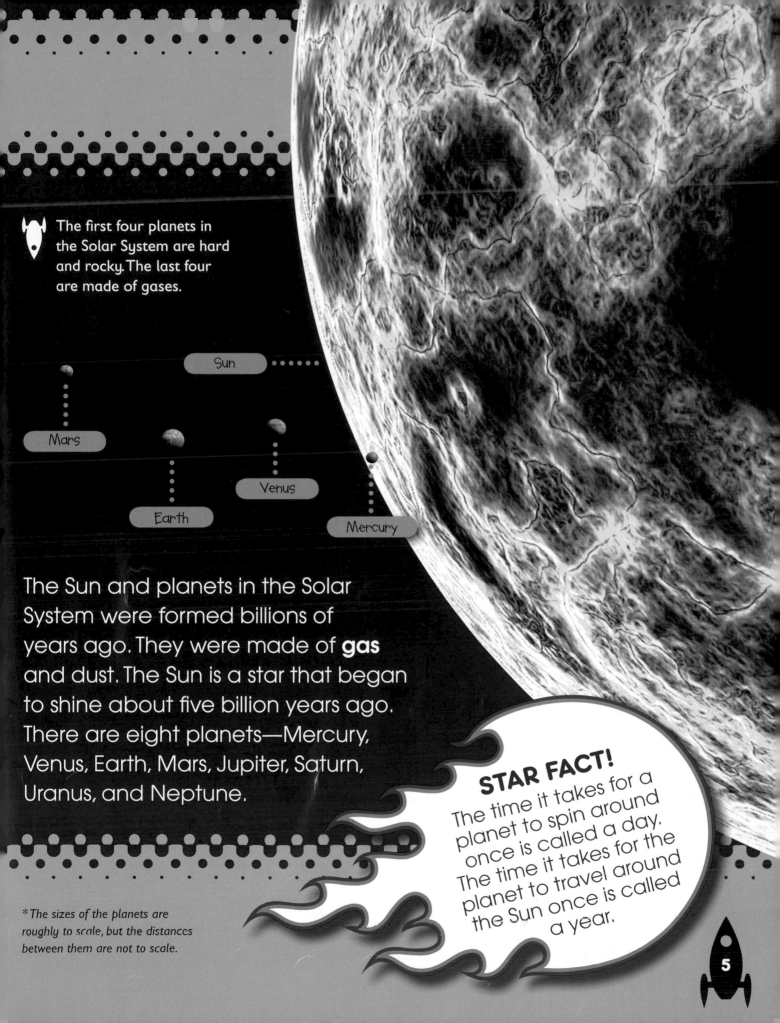

The first four planets in the Solar System are hard and rocky. The last four are made of gases.

Sun

Mars

Venus

Earth

Mercury

The Sun and planets in the Solar System were formed billions of years ago. They were made of **gas** and dust. The Sun is a star that began to shine about five billion years ago. There are eight planets—Mercury, Venus, Earth, Mars, Jupiter, Saturn, Uranus, and Neptune.

*The sizes of the planets are roughly to scale, but the distances between them are not to scale.

STAR FACT!
The time it takes for a planet to spin around once is called a day. The time it takes for the planet to travel around the Sun once is called a year.

Mercury

Mercury is the closest planet to the Sun.
It is also the smallest planet in the Solar System,
slightly bigger than Earth's Moon. Mercury does
not have a moon of its own.

Mercury   Venus   Earth

Mercury is a dry, rocky planet. Its surface
is covered in holes called **craters**. The
craters were made when meteors and
comets crashed into the planet.

 Mercury and Venus
are both hard, rocky
planets, but they are very
different from each other.

As Mercury is so close to the Sun, the temperatures there get very hot during daytime, but it also gets very cold at nighttime!

STAR FACT!
Mercury is named after the speedy Roman messenger god because it's a fast-moving planet! It travels at 30 miles a second!

Mercury looks like the Moon. The craters are billions of years old. They were made when the Solar System formed.

7

Hot and cold

Mercury is unusual because it spins so slowly.

A day on Mercury is 176 Earth days. Mercury travels around the Sun once every 88 days, so a year on Mercury is only 88 Earth days—the day is twice as long as the year!

 On Mercury, there is daylight for 88 days and then darkness for 88 days.

STAR FACT!
The surface of Mercury is wrinkled. When the core, or middle, cooled, the planet shrank—just like a balloon that has lost its air.

Mercury gets very hot during the 88 days of sunlight. The temperature can reach 800 degrees Fahrenheit —so hot that it could melt **lead**.

When the Sun sets, Mercury cools down to -290 degrees Fahrenheit. If Earth were ever to get that cold, the air would start to turn from gas into liquid.

The dark side of Mercury is so dark that nothing can be seen. In 2008, scientists saw a complete close-up of Mercury for the first time, including the dark side.

A cratered world

Mercury is almost completely covered in craters.

Some of the deep craters near Mercury's north pole never get any sunlight. Scientists think that they might have found ice in these craters, even though Mercury is so close to the Sun.

The biggest crater is Caloris Basin. It is 960 miles across and one mile deep.

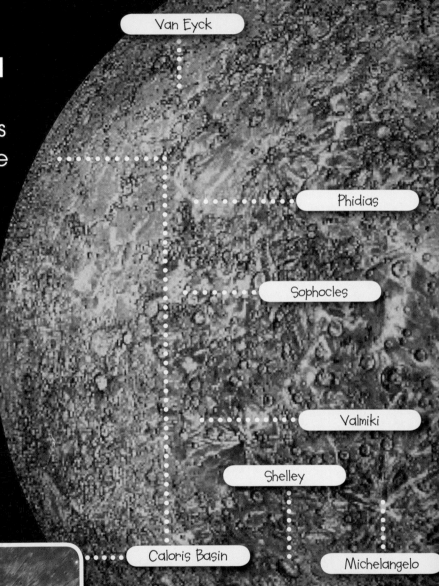

Van Eyck

Phidias

Sophocles

Valmiki

Shelley

Caloris Basin

Michelangelo

Wagner

Bach

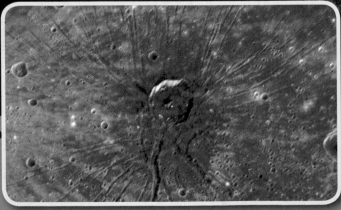

The "spider" crater inside Caloris Basin has lots of grooves that look like spiders' legs.

Spacecraft have taken pictures of Mercury's wrinkled, cratered surface.

STAR FACT!
The craters on Mercury are named after famous writers, artists, and composers, such as Shelley, Renoir, and Wagner.

Vivaldi

Renoir

Chekhov

Schubert

Many of the craters were made when the planet was hit by an asteroid or comet, but some were made by **volcanoes**. **Space probes** have also taken pictures of smooth areas called **plains**, similar to the "seas" on the Moon.

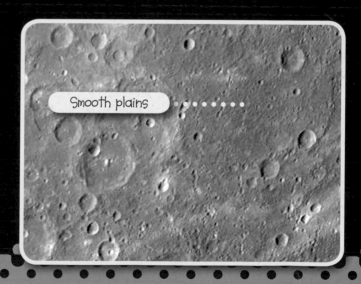

Smooth plains

Melting ice

Find out if ice melts more quickly in sunlight or in shade. Take two ice cubes out of the freezer. Put one on a plate in the sunlight. Put one on a plate in the shade. Which one melts first?

Mercury's plains can be smooth and flat, or filled with craters.

To explore the planets, scientists often use space probes.
Space probes can either fly past or orbit a planet. Some space probes land on the surface of the rocky planets or moons.

STAR FACT!
The **Hubble Space Telescope** cannot take pictures of Mercury because the planet is too close to the Sun.

Mercury Messenger was launched in 2004. It will pass Mercury three times before it can start orbiting the planet in 2011.

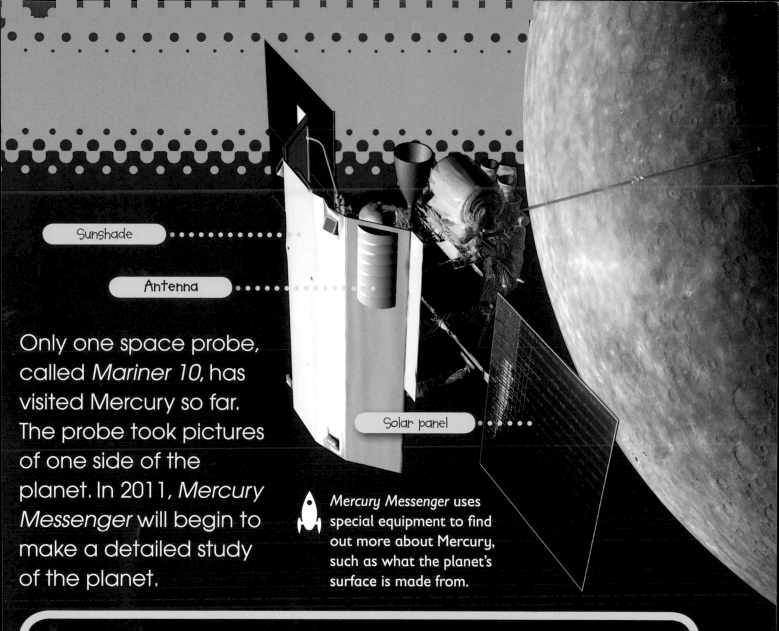

Sunshade

Antenna

Solar panel

Only one space probe, called *Mariner 10*, has visited Mercury so far. The probe took pictures of one side of the planet. In 2011, *Mercury Messenger* will begin to make a detailed study of the planet.

Mercury Messenger uses special equipment to find out more about Mercury, such as what the planet's surface is made from.

Venus has been visited by 20 space probes and is the most visited planet in the Solar System. *Venus Express* is there now. It is looking at Venus' clouds and surface.

 Venus Express reached Venus in 2006. Its wings are **solar panels** that collect sunlight to provide power for the spacecraft.

Venus

Venus is the second planet from the Sun.

It orbits the Sun between Mercury and Earth. Venus is about the same size as Earth, but looks very different. Like Mercury, it is a planet without a moon.

Venus was the first planet ever to be visited and landed on by a space probe. The surface of Venus is very smooth—it does not have many craters.

Finding Venus

You can see Venus either in the morning or in the evening.

The Evening Star

Venus is the first bright light you see after the Sun sets.

The Morning Star

Venus is the last bright light you see before the Sun rises.

  Pictures have been made of Venus to show what it would look like if it had no clouds.

The clouds around Venus are so thick that scientists use special instruments to see the surface.

Venus can be seen in the sky if it is not too close to the Sun. It looks like a very bright star that does not twinkle.

Moon

Venus

 After the Sun and the Moon, Venus is the brightest object in the sky. It is so bright that it can sometimes be seen when there are no stars in the sky.

Hot, hot, hot

A planet warms up when it is in sunlight.

The closer a planet is to the Sun, the warmer the sunlight is. Mercury should be the hottest planet, but Venus gets hotter than Mercury, even though it is farther from the Sun!

Mercury has almost no atmosphere because wind from the Sun sweeps it all away.

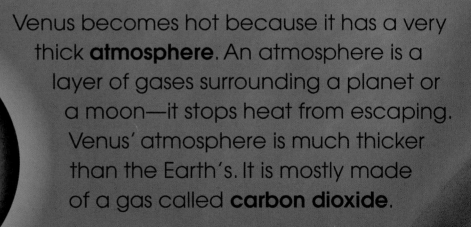

Venus becomes hot because it has a very thick **atmosphere**. An atmosphere is a layer of gases surrounding a planet or a moon—it stops heat from escaping. Venus' atmosphere is much thicker than the Earth's. It is mostly made of a gas called **carbon dioxide**.

It is always cloudy on Venus! The clouds on Venus are not made of water—they are made of acid.

Using balloons is one of the best ways to explore Venus. In the 1980s, balloons measured the winds and temperature of the planet.

Balloon

Volcano

Probe

STAR FACT!
The atmosphere on Venus is so thick that the pressure is like being under 3,000 feet of water—or being squashed by a pile of 15 tanks!

VAP

Crossing the Sun

Sometimes Venus passes between the Sun and Earth. This is called a **transit** and can actually be seen from Earth. The planet appears as a small dot crossing the face of the Sun!

 Transits occur when a planet moves directly between the Sun and Earth. Only Mercury and Venus can transit the Sun.

STAR FACT!
Mercury transits happen quite often—about 13 times in 100 years. The last transit took place on November 8, 2006.

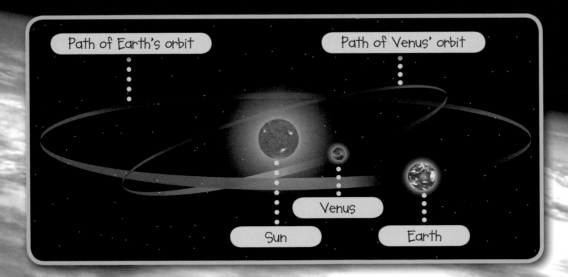

Path of Earth's orbit

Path of Venus' orbit

Earth

Venus

Sun

Earth

Sun

Venus

The planet blocks out a circle of sunlight and so it looks like a black dot on the face of the Sun.

Transits of Venus only take place every few hundred years—and then two happen within eight years! Scientists can now predict when transits will appear.

You must use special glasses to look at the Sun. They block out all the dangerous rays.

The last transit of Venus was on June 8, 2004—it lasted for six hours. The next transit will be on June 5 to 6, 2012. You must wear special glasses because looking at the Sun can damage your eyes.

Volcanoes

As Venus is so cloudy, we cannot see the surface. However, scientists discovered that underneath the clouds, Venus has lots of volcanoes.

 Hot, runny rock called **magma** came up from volcanoes on Venus. It came to the surface as **lava** and cooled to give Venus a smooth surface.

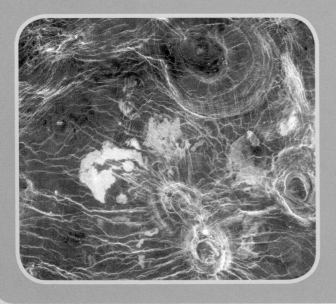

Venus has more volcanoes than any other planet in the Solar System—more than 1,600 major volcanoes have been discovered. Most of the volcanoes on Venus are probably **inactive**.

 On Venus, the unusual "spider" shapes are large volcanic holes surrounded by many cracks.

The biggest volcano on Venus is Maat Mons. It is 5 miles in height—almost as tall as Mount Everest. The *Magellan* probe has seen signs that may mean Maat Mons is still active.

 The *Magellan* probe spent more than four years orbiting Venus to create a map of the planet's surface.

Glossary

Antenna
A wire that is used for receiving radio and television signals.

Asteroid
A large lump of rock, too small to be a planet or dwarf planet.

Astronaut
A person who travels in space.

Atmosphere
A layer of gases around a planet or moon.

Carbon dioxide
Colorless gas needed by plants to grow.

Comet
An object in space made of rock and ice.

Crater
A hole made on the surface of a planet or moon by an asteroid or comet.

Gas
A substance, such as air, that is not solid or liquid. Gas cannot usually be seen.

Gravity
Attractive pulling force between any massive objects.

Hubble Space Telescope
A telescope that is orbiting the Earth.

Inactive (volcano)
A volcano that does not erupt any more.

Lava
Molten, or liquid, rock that has cooled and turned into a solid.

Lead
A soft, heavy, gray metal.

Magma
Hot, runny rock from the middle of a planet or moon.

Meteor
A glowing trail in the sky left by a small piece of rock from space.

Orbit
The path of one body around another, such as a planet around the Sun.

Plain
An area of smooth, flat land.

Solar panel
A panel that changes the Sun's energy into electricity or heat.

Spacecraft
A vehicle that travels in space.

Space probe
A spacecraft without people on board.

Transit
When Mercury or Venus passes across the face of the Sun.

Volcano
A place where magma comes to the surface.

Index

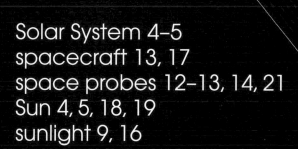

Notes for parents and teachers

- Venus can be seen most easily either around sunrise or in the early evening. Observing information can be found at www.skyandtelescope.com/observing/ataglance*.

- Venus stays hot because the atmosphere traps heat from the Sun. This is a good opportunity to discuss the common misconception that we get cold because we let cold in. In fact, we get cold because we let heat escape. Talk about which parts of a room are warm and cold. Discuss why this might be.

- Heat energy moves by conduction (from object to object – a metal spoon gets hot when it is in a hot drink), convection (when the object itself moves – warm air moving around a room), and radiation (energy transported by waves, such as sunlight).

- You can also talk about what materials are best at keeping us warm. Why is a coat or duvet better at keeping us warm than a T-shirt or a thin sheet? Hot air expands and rises, so would normally move away from our bodies (convection). Fluffy materials trap the warm air, and stop it moving away from our body.

- Finding ice on Mercury sounds impossible, as it is so close to the Sun. During its long day, Mercury can get much hotter than boiling water. However, some very deep craters near Mercury's north pole are always in shadow. As Mercury's atmosphere is very thin, it does not help to keep the planet warm.

- Observing Mercury is difficult because it is never far from the Sun. The Hubble Space Telescope cannot take pictures of Mercury because it is so close to the Sun.

- A day (sunrise to sunrise) on Mercury lasts 176 Earth days. This is twice as long as it takes Mercury to go around the Sun! The planet turns so slowly, that when *Mariner 10* flew by, the probe only saw just under half of the surface. The other half was too dark to see.